ice dancing

Anna Claybourne

First published in 2011 by Wayland

Copyright © Wayland 2011

Wayland
Hachette Children's Books
338 Euston Road
London NW1 3BH

Wayland Australia
Level 17/207 Kent Street
Sydney NSW 2000

Concept by Joyce Bentley

Commissioned by Debbie Foy and
Rasha Elsaeed

Produced for Wayland by Calcium
Designer: Paul Myerscough
Editor: Sarah Eason

British Library Cataloguing in Publication Data

Claybourne, Anna.
  Ice dancing : the skaters, the stars, the glitz. —
  (Dance culture)(Radar)
  1. Ice dancing—Juvenile literature. 2. Ice dancers
  —Juvenile literature. 3. Figure skating—Juvenile
  literature. 4. Figure skaters—Juvenile literature.
  I. Title II. Series
  796.9'12-dc22

SBN: 978 0 7502 6456 3

Printed in China

Wayland is a division of Hachette Children's Books,
an Hachette UK company.

www.hachette.co.uk

Acknowledgements: Alamy: Amoret Tanner 7;
Corbis: Jean-Yves Ruszniewski/TempSport;
Stewart Feinstein: 20–21, 26–27; Flickr: Dave
Wharton Photography 4–5; Philip Rees
Photography: 14; Shutterstock: Almotional 31,
Diego Barbieri 9, 12cl, 25tr, Galina Barskaya
25bc, Olga Besnard 1, 12bl, 22–23, 24r, 25tl,
Songguan Deng 19, Gertan 10, André
Klaassen 13tl, Klaus Rainer Krieger 18, Testing
cover, 6, 13bl, 13cr, 16br, 16tr, Valeria73 17;
Wikipedia: Caroline Paré 3br.

cover stories

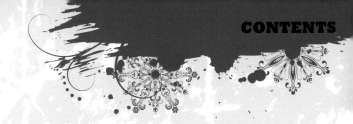

the**people**

the**moves**

the**talk**

DANCING ON THE ICE!

Graceful dance moves, aerial jumps and lifts, and incredibly fast spins make figure skating challenging and impressive to watch. Performing on the ice requires strength and fitness, perfect timing and highly expressive body movements.

Figure skating disciplines include freestyle, pairs, ice dance and synchronised skating. Each has its own special rules, techniques and skills.

Freestyle

Energetic and exciting, freestyle skating is full of spectacular jumps and spins. Freestyle is performed by a solo (singles) skater.

Pairs

Male and female skaters perform together in pairs skating. They can skate together or apart, but their movements, including jumps and spins, must be perfectly synchronised, with matching footwork, body shapes and even facial expressions!

Ice dance

Without the dramatic spins and lifts of freestyle and pairs skating, ice dancers perform ballroom-style moves on the ice. Music is very important, with skaters telling a story through their flowing body shapes and constant changes of direction.

Synchronised skating

This style can involve up to 20 skaters at one time performing perfectly synchronised dance routines on the ice.

Celebrity skating!

Reality TV ice dancing shows have been a huge hit around the world, attracting millions of viewers. Celebrities are partnered with professional skaters and, in the case of UK's *Dancing On Ice*, are trained by the former Olympic champions Jayne Torvill and Christopher Dean. From Italy to Chile, ice dancing shows have encouraged many people – young and old – to get their skates on and head to an ice rink!

THE STORY OF SKATING

The oldest pair of skates dates back to about 3000 BCE, and was found at the bottom of a lake in Switzerland. Made from the leg bones of large animals, holes were made at each end of the bone, and leather straps were used to tie the skates on.

Skates get an update

In the fourteenth century, the Dutch started using wooden skates with flat pieces of iron attached to the bottom. They were tied to the shoes with leather straps, and skaters would push themselves across the ice with a long pole. Two hundred years later, a narrow metal blade was added, allowing the skater to push and glide with his feet without using a pole.

The first skating club

The world's first skating club was formed almost 300 years ago in Edinburgh, Scotland. Entry was easy by today's standards — candidates had to skate simple shapes (or 'figures') and jump over three hats piled on top of each other!

Trailblazer

US ballet dancer and skater Jackson Haines is credited with being the man who invented modern figure skating in the 1860s. Wearing the skates he had invented (with blades screwed directly into the soles of his boots), Haines entertained crowds with his athletic jumps and spins. His speciality, the sit spin, is one of the basic spin types still used today.

Waltzing on ice

The discipline of ice dance developed as a sport in the 1930s, with the first demonstrations of dances such as the tango, foxtrot and Viennese waltz performed on ice. Ice dance has a long history in the UK – with 12 of the first 16 Ice Dance World Championships held there.

A series of 'mini ice ages' during the nineteenth century contributed to the Victorians' love of skating. People flocked to skate on Britain's frozen lakes.

Olympic golds

Between 1976 and 1984, Britain won three Olympic skating gold medals. The success of skaters John Curry in 1976, Robin Cousins in 1980, and the pair Jayne Torvill and Christopher Dean in 1984 had a powerful impact on young skaters all over the world. Torvill and Dean earned a record-breaking 12 perfect 6.0 marks for their memorable performance of Ravel's *Bolero*.

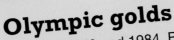

Eastern promise

Ice skating has seen a huge surge in popularity in Asia, particularly in Japan, China and South Korea. At the 2010 World Figure Skating Championships in Italy, China took the gold in the pairs skating, and Japan took gold in the men's and ladies' singles. At the 2010 Winter Olympics, Mao Asada of Japan became the first woman to land three triple axel jumps in the same competition.

SPICE UP THE ICE!

Are you looking for a hobby that combines dance, drama, speed, skill and strength? Try figure skating! Here are some of the reasons why you should get your skates on.

2

Ice skating is fantastic exercise. One hour performing on the ice is the equivalent of an 8-kilometre run, raising your heart rate, working your stomach muscles, strengthening your thighs, and even exercising your shoulders and upper arms. Skating also improves your balance, and increases your stamina, too.

1

The best ice dancers come alive in front of an audience, losing themselves in the music and movement, and creating a wonderful spectacle. If you enjoy performing, and love dressing up in colourful, eye-catching outfits, this is the hobby for you!

3

Figure skating is a year-round hobby. During the winter months there are many outdoor rinks that are great places to go and have fun with your friends. For the rest of the year, you can head indoors to your local ice rink. The fun never has to stop!

Type 'ice skating Olympics' into www.youtube.com to watch the professionals in action.

4 Work hard and keep practising, and you could turn a fun hobby into an exciting career. Apart from competing in events such as the World Championships and Winter Olympics, professional skaters perform around the world in exhibitions, travelling ice shows or even on television. Imagine being paid to do something you love!

5 Performing on the ice is something you can do for a lifetime. Skaters as young as 15 have won Olympic medals, and ice dance is a brilliant way for older people to stay fit and have fun. Even though some of the falls look spectacular, it's a hobby with relatively few injuries.

Ice skating can be anything you want it to be – fast, exciting and physical, or graceful, controlled and glamorous. Skaters can go it alone, pair up with a partner, or even become part of a huge synchronised team. There's something for everyone to enjoy. What are you waiting for? Spice up the ice!

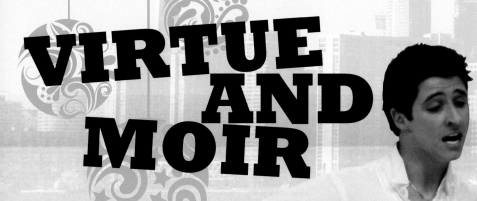

VIRTUE AND MOIR

Ice skate sweethearts

Tessa and Scott set
the ice on fire with their
figure skating magic.

Type 'Winter Olympics 2010 Tessa and Scott' into www.youtube.com to see the champions burn up the ice.

THE STATS
Name: Tessa Virtue
Born: 17 May 1989
Place of birth: London, Ontario, Canada
Job: Competitive ice skater

THE STATS
Name: Scott Moir
Born: 2 September 1987
Place of birth: London, Ontario, Canada
Job: Competitive ice skater

First meeting

Tessa was just seven and Scott was nine years old when they first began skating together. Scott's family ran an ice skating camp, and his aunt paired him with Tessa for competitions. Scott was really into ice hockey and ice skating, but when the time came, he chose to concentrate on skating – and started down a path to ice rink super-stardom!

Junior champs

It soon became clear that Scott and Tessa were something special. As teenagers, they competed at junior level and won ten gold medals, three silvers and three bronzes at Canadian and world championships – including gold at the Junior World Championships in 2006.

Moving on up

From 2006, Tessa and Scott competed at senior level. By the end of the 2009-2010 season, they had won 17 medals at international and national level – nine of them gold! They came first in Ice Dancing in the Canadian Figure Skating Championships three times in a row, becoming celebrities in Canada.

Olympic gold

Tessa and Scott made their Olympic debut at the 2010 Winter Olympics in Vancouver, Canada. Stunning the home audience with a flawless and breathtakingly beautiful free dance, Canada's 'ice skating sweethearts' became the first ice dancers to win gold at their very first Olympic games.

THE SPINS

layback spin

camel spin

From spectacular uprights to complicated camels, spins are used to add drama and grace to a performance. Here are some of the most popular.

Layback spin

This graceful upright spin is usually performed by a female skater. The hips are pushed forward, allowing the back to bend. The skater extends her head and neck while supporting her weight on one leg and lifting the free leg behind her. In the spin shown left, the arms are raised in a ballet-like pose.

Camel spin

In this spin, the body forms a T-shape where the free leg is stretched out behind, while the skater balances on the spinning leg. The camel spin requires good technique, timing and balance.

Biellmann spin

This breathtaking upright move starts with the skater spinning with one leg raised. The skater bends to the side to take hold of the blade with one hand and pulls the leg backwards and up. She then holds the blade with both hands to pull it up behind the head. This spin requires great flexibility.

Sit spin

This is a spin performed in a 'sitting' position. The skater's rear should not be higher than the level of the supporting knee. The free leg is usually extended out in front. The upper part of the spinning leg must be parallel to the ice.

Haircutter spin

This is a variation of the layback spin, but the free skate is brought towards the head. The blade gets close enough to 'cut' the skater's hair!

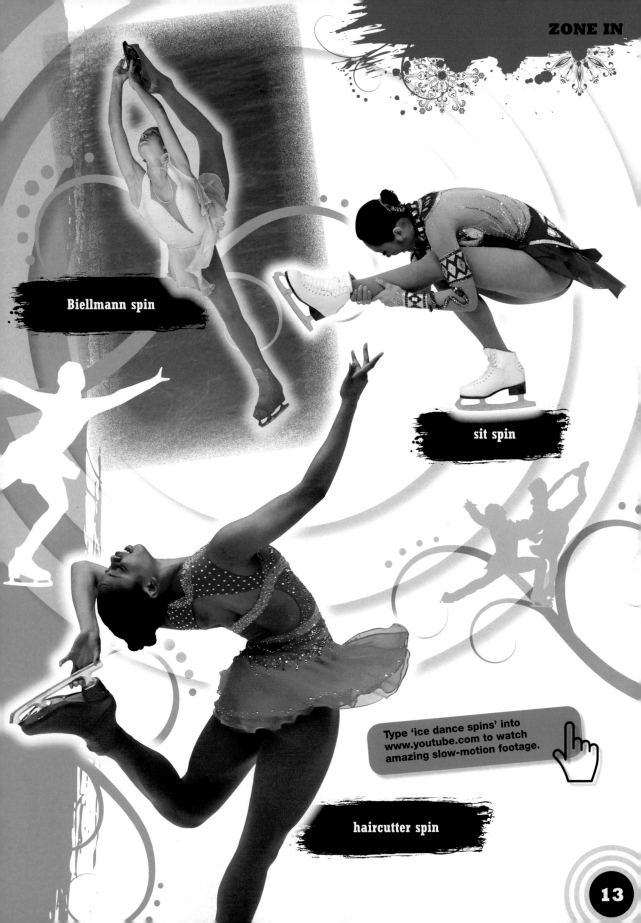

Biellmann spin

sit spin

haircutter spin

Type 'ice dance spins' into www.youtube.com to watch amazing slow-motion footage.

13

PARTY ON ICE

My story by Zoe Rees

My very first skating memories are quite embarrassing! My friends were into ice skating birthday parties and it seemed like everyone could skate except me. I was so bad my mum had to hold my hand and help me round the rink! I was determined to get better though, and at ten years old I started lessons.

The first stage was joining a beginners' course at my local rink. The idea was you mastered the basics one level at a time. When you passed, you moved on to the next level. I picked things up quickly, and soon felt much more confident on the ice. When I was 11, I won a 'Most Improved Skater' award from my club. I'd only been learning for a year, and so winning was the best feeling ever.

Now I'm at the rink four times a week for up to four hours each time! I'm practising for skating exams. At the moment I'm mastering double jumps! I really want to be a coach one day. That's something I'm working towards now.

Figure skating has taught me that hard work and determination pay off. If you get something wrong, you just have to pick yourself up and keep on trying. Skating's a brilliant hobby that has helped me to make lots of great friends, and keep me really fit. And if anyone invites me to a party on ice these days, I let mum stay at home!

ICE SPEAK

Don't head to the rink until you've read Radar's ice speak guide!

blade
the metal part of a skate that makes contact with the ice

double axel
a jump with a forward take off. The skater does two and a half spins in the air and lands facing backwards

double jump
a jump that involves two rotations in the air before landing

edge work
precise footwork on skates, performed on the edges of the blade

edges
the fine ridges of steel on either side of a skate blade

figure skating
an artisic sport which includes several disciplines that showcase jumps, dances, lifts, spins and figures

free dance
an ice dance programme in which the dancers choose their music and make up their own routine and moves

free programme
a competition performance that lasts four minutes and 30 seconds for men. For women and juniors it is four minutes

freestyle
a figure skating discipline in which skaters are free to add lifts, spins and jumps to their programmes

ice dance
a figure skating discipline in which a man and a woman perform versions of ballroom dances on ice

pairs
when a male and female skater perform together

plyometrics
a type of exercise designed to produce fast, powerful movements. It helps skaters perform somersaults and spins

quad/ quadruple
a jump in which the skater spins around four times in the air before landing

rink
an indoor or outdoor expanse of ice used for ice skating

short programme
a competition performance that lasts no longer than two minutes and 50 seconds

singles
solo skating

split scissor
an aerial pose where the legs are open like a pair of scissors

step sequences
quick changes of direction and foot movements used to travel around the ice

stroking
a term used to describe moving from one skate to the other to travel across the ice

triple axel
a jump with a forward take off. The skater does three and a half spins in the air and lands facing backwards

GLOSSARY

BCE
stands for 'before common era', a term used to describe the period of time before the death of Jesus Christ

complex carbohydrates
energy-giving foods such as bread, rice and pasta

consecutive
following straight on from a previous event

finale
the end part of a performance

ice age
a time when parts of the Earth became dramatically colder and were covered with snow and ice

invigorate
to be filled with energy

momentum
an impelling force or strength of movement

seasonal
happening only at certain times of the year

synchronise
when body movements are coordinated, often in time to music

THE NEW ICE AGE

In city centres and tourist spots around the world, you are likely to find a temporary ice rink nearby. Where did the idea come from, and what effect is it having on the popularity of skating? Read on to find out...

The ice skating bug means that heading to a rink for a weekend skate has become a common pastime for many people.

Starting the trend

The granddaddy of all outdoor skating venues is The Rink at the Rockefeller Centre in New York, USA. Built in 1936, it attracts a quarter of a million people every winter! Skaters also flock to the open air Wollman Rink in the city's famous Central Park.

In the UK, the impressive eighteenth-century Somerset House in London is credited with starting the outdoor ice rink craze back in 2000. For fun-loving families the world over, a trip to a magical outdoor ice rink has become as traditional as a pantomime or Christmas crackers.

Crowd-pulling fun!

Today's seasonal rinks can cost up to £300,000 to build and maintain. Nevertheless, their numbers keep growing around the world. Today there are rinks in San Francisco's Union Square, at Boston's Common Frog Pond, Berlin's Potsdamer Platz and even at the Eiffel Tower in Paris! Local businesses see the rinks as a great way to attract crowds who will also do a spot of shopping, eating and drinking when they take off their skates.

The ice bug

Seasonal ice rinks are here to stay. According to Matt Howes, who runs the UK's largest supplier of seasonal rinks, 'Instead of waiting for people to come to the sport, we took the sport to the people.' The result of this improved access to ice rinks is that more people are being bitten by the skating bug. If you pull on a pair of skates for the first time under the moonlight, overlooked by wonderful historical buildings, top tourist spots, or a buzzing city centre, skating becomes magic, fantasy and fun! And the chances are you'll want to go back again and again.

With the stunning cityscape of New York in the background, the Wollman Rink is popular with tourists and New Yorkers alike.

Type 'Somerset House skate' into www.youtube.com to see skaters enjoying a magical Christmas on ice!

A WEEK IN THE LIFE OF INTERNATIONAL SKATER

JONO PARTRIDGE

blog   **news**   **events**

Monday

I ate an energy-packed breakfast – five eggs, porridge and a glass of milk – before heading to the ice rink. After 45 minutes working on spins, I ran through my free programme. My practice sessions are always based around the two routines we perform at competitions – the short programme and the free programme. Then I headed to the gym for some strength work.

Tuesday

My training today focused on jumps, spins and step sequences. After doing my steps it was back home for a healthy dinner – fish, brown rice and steamed vegetables. My diet is based around protein and complex carbohydrates for energy.

Wednesday

I was on the ice by 9.00am today to practise my jumps. It's best to get to the rink when the ice has just been resurfaced – fresh ice is more 'springy' and far

blog   news   events

better for jumping. Where I train in Colorado, USA, the ice is resurfaced every 45 minutes. Here in the UK, it's more like once a day.

Thursday

Tomorrow is competition day! I had four sessions on the ice today of 45 minutes each. I focused on the most difficult parts from each programme. I wanted everything to be perfect – like I could do it in my sleep! Then I did three 20-minute stretching sessions to warm down and stay flexible.

Friday

The big day's finally here! I had a stretching session in the morning and worked through my jumps in my head. They are the hardest things to get right. The triple axel is the hardest jump in the world! My short programme went well, and my score was a personal best so I felt good.

Saturday

Today was the free programme competition. I didn't skate as well as I know I can. My nerves got to me, and I just didn't feel loose. It was frustrating because the moves were coming out perfectly in practice all week! But I still ended the competition with a new personal best score, which was great. On Monday morning I'll start all over again!

COMPETITION FEVER!

You take a deep breath and move towards the centre of the ice. A hush falls over the crowd, the lights go down and the judges straighten in their seats. You strike your starting pose, eyes down, feet turned out, arms by your sides. The lights sparkle on your costume like a thousand tiny diamonds. You're as still as a statue, but your heart pounds in your chest like a drum. It's time to begin.

Glassy rink

You hear the first few notes of the music. It's lively and exhilarating, perfect for the routine you've been practising for months. The hours you've spent on the ice immediately kick in, and your body responds as if by remote control – driven by the sounds. The ice is fresh, your blades are sharp and your body feels strong and supple. It's like you're gliding on glass as you work your way around the rink.

Ice magic

You feel the cool air hit your face and it invigorates you, sending a magical feeling flowing through your veins, and making your pulse race. Every pore in your body is working toward one goal, the ultimate performance. It's intense, like you're floating on air. You turn and spin with ease, then glide beautifully like a graceful swan. The audience and judges drift away from your mind as you move towards your finale.

Skate gold

The next thing you know you're lifting off, soaring, spinning, once, twice, three times! Time stands still and there is only you, the air, the ice and the moment. You land perfectly. All around you there is the sight and sound of a thousand camera flashes. Then the noise starts to build. The sound of clapping and cheering fills your ears, and brings tears to your eyes. You've done it – a gold medal for a winning performance.

THE LIFTS AND JUMPS

Lifts and jumps are an important part of figure skating. Get them right, and you add drama, excitement and judges' points to your routine. Here are just a few the experts use.

Throw jump

This is a dramatic pairs move, in which the man 'throws' the woman into the air. She spins and lands on her own.

Lasso lift

In this lift, the couple begin by holding hands as they skate. The man then lifts the woman around his back and above his head (as though he is swinging a lasso!).

Twist lift

This pairs move starts with the couple skating backwards. The man holds the woman around the waist, lifts her off the ice and throws her into the air. The woman spins horizontally and is then caught around the waist and lowered back to the ice.

Star lift

In this spectacular lift, the man puts his hand on his partner's hip and lifts her above his head. The man holds one of his partner's hands as he lifts her in the air – he can then let go so that he holds the woman up with just one hand. She positions her arms and legs in a 'split scissor' position to make a 'star' shape.

throw jump

lasso lift

twist lift

star lift

STEWART FEINSTEIN

Leading international figure skating coach, Stewart trains skaters in London and Colorado Springs, USA. He turned professional at 21, and has toured with the famous *Holiday On Ice* show. Read on to get the low-down on how to be a skating star.

How did you get into skating?

I started at 13, and everything about it fascinated me. I loved what you can do on the ice, and I couldn't get enough of it! In my teens, I began having one-to-one lessons and in my early twenties I turned professional by touring Europe in *Operatta On Ice*.

What makes a top skater?

Firstly, you have to have dedication. Skating is not a sport you can learn quickly. Secondly, you need to believe in yourself. Jumps require mental ability – if you don't succeed at first, you have to pick yourself up and try again until you do.

How can I fall over without hurting myself?

Falls are all part of skating, but if you feel that you're going to fall, try and relax into it. If you stiffen up, you are more likely to hurt yourself. Just imagine you're falling onto a soft carpet. Remember to tuck your fingers in – you don't want another skater going over them!

Stewart (right) with British and international medalist Jono Partridge (see pages 20–21).

What's your favourite skating style?

I'd have to say freestyle. Successful freestyle skaters have to keep pushing the boundaries of their abilities – at top level you will see skaters perform jumps such as a triple axel and a quadruple jump in a programme. You can't afford to stand still.

What's the first thing you teach absolute beginners?

It sounds funny, but I teach them to stand on the ice with heels touching in a V shape, keeping their body weight over their feet, and their knees bent. They then start lifting their feet up and down and moving forwards. They can then learn to push off on the inside of the blade to give power to their forward movement.

Why do skaters wear such glamorous outfits?

Dancing on the ice in particular is all about drama and storytelling. A skater's costume plays an important role in helping to tell a story. It combines with the spins, jumps and steps to make a complete performance.

27

THE BACKFLIP

The backflip is a move that brings the audience to its feet. Former gymnast and European freestyle skater Surya Bonaly (pictured here) is famous for landing the backflip on just one foot. She is one of the few skaters in the world able to do this.

Essential technique

- Speed before take off
- Momentum during somersault
- Precise landing

How it's done

1. The skater starts by moving backwards. She begins at one end of the rink to build up speed.
2. Keeping one foot on the ice, she swings the other leg back behind her, then brings it forward again quickly.

The momentum starts to tip her body backwards.

3. As she begins to somersault, the skater rotates as quickly as she can. She lands on the same leg she was skating on before the backflip.

Type 'Surya Bonaly backflip' into www.youtube.com to see her amazing backflip in action!

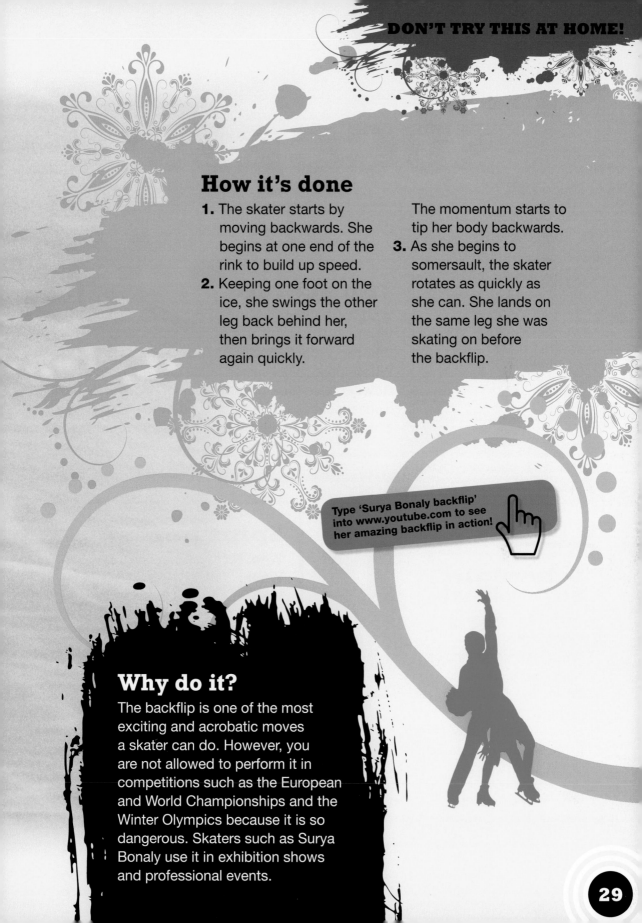

Why do it?

The backflip is one of the most exciting and acrobatic moves a skater can do. However, you are not allowed to perform it in competitions such as the European and World Championships and the Winter Olympics because it is so dangerous. Skaters such as Surya Bonaly use it in exhibition shows and professional events.

SKATE SUCCESS!

Check out the youngest, fastest and most spectacular in our round-up...

Top scorer!

Who: Yu-Na Kim
When: 2010
Where: Winter Olympics, Vancouver, Canada
What: Most points scored in the Winter Olympics
How: Entered the Guinness Book of Records for the highest points total ever achieved by a female skater at the Olympics, with an amazing 228.56 score!

Schoolgirl superstar!

Who: Tara Lipinski
When: 1998
Where: Winter Olympics, Nagano, Japan
What: Youngest individual Olympic medallist
How: Won the ladies singles figure skating gold medal at just 15!

Spins per min!

Who: Natalia Kanounnikova
When: 2007
Where: The Rink, Rockefeller Centre, New York, USA
What: Fastest spin
How: Broke the world record for the fastest spin ever recorded – 308 revolutions per minute. That's over five spins per second!

Champ jumper!

Who: Kurt Browning
When: 1988
Where: The World Championships, Budapest, Hungary
What: First quadruple jump landed in a competition
How: Landed the first ever competitive 'quad' – in which a skater spins four times before landing!

Golden boy!

Who: Gillis Grafström
When: 1928
Where: St Moritz, Switzerland
What: Three consecutive gold medals
How: Won three gold medals in men's figure skating at consecutive Olympics – from 1920 to 1928. At his final Winter Olympics in 1932, he collided with a photographer on the ice and still managed to win a silver!

Super spins!

Who: Lucinda Ruh
When: 2003
Where: Chelsea Piers Sky Rink, New York City, USA
What: Most continuous spins on one foot
How: Set a new world record by rotating an impressive 115 times on live TV!

GET YOUR SKATES ON!

People to talk to

Perhaps you've experienced the exhilaration of gliding across the ice with a group of friends, but now you're keen to learn more. Radar can show you the way!

NISA

To find an ice rink and a 'Learn to Skate' course near you, head straight to:
www.national-ice-centre.com

Radar expert

If you want to be coached by ice skating supremo, Stewart Feinstein, you can contact him at Lee Valley Park ice rink:
www.leevalleypark.org.uk

Champ talk

Check out the figure skating news and interviews with champion skaters at:
www.figureskatersonline.com

DVDs, Reads & Apps

Pick up some great tips and pointers from coach Heather Luscombe on her 2010 DVD *Beginning Ice Skating.*

Want to read more about skating? For great fiction reads try:
Skating School by Linda Chapman (Puffin, 2010)

Skate School by Kay Woodward (Usborne, 2009)

For facts and stats pick up:
Winter Olympic Sports: Figure Skating by Joseph Gustaitis (Crabtree, 2009)

Skate straight over to iTunes for the *SportsVideo: Ice Skating* app
www.itunes.com

INDEX

your mission:
To seek out more
cool Radar reads...

radar

BOARD SPORTS
theboarders
thetricks
thegear
978 0 7502 6459 4

FREE RUNNING
therunners
themoves
thefreedom
978 0 7502 6458 7

FREESTYLE BMX
thebikers
thestunts
thebuzz
978 0 7502 6457 0

STREET FOOTBALL
theplayers
theskills
thegames
978 0 7502 6460 0

More Radar titles coming soon!

Graffiti Culture	Being a Pro Footballer
Street Art	Being a DJ
Cool Brands	Being a Stuntman
Body Decoration	Being a Snowboarder
	Being a Model
The Armed Services	Being a Formula 1 Racing Driver
The Special Forces	Celebrity Make-up Artist
Undercover Operations	Celebrity Fashion Stylist
Police Forensics	Celebrity Photographer

Are you on the Radar?